FOUR BITS
Fifty 50-Word Pieces

by Jason Stanizzi

FOUR BITS
Fifty 50-Word Pieces

John L. Stanizzi

GRAYSON BOOKS
West Hartford, CT
www.GraysonBooks.com

Four Bits
Copyright © 2018 by John L. Stanizzi
Library of Congress Control Number: 2018958082
ISBN: 978-0-9994327-5-4
published by Grayson Books
West Hartford, CT
printed in the USA

Interior & Cover Design: Cindy Mercier
Cover Photo: John L. Stanizzi

For Carol, and as always, for Clem.

ACKNOWLEDGEMENTS

Thanks to the following publications for first publishing these works.

Abstract Magazine TV: "Before Rain, Before Dawn"

after the pause: "I Still Wonder If Anyone Saw"

Ariel: "Heat's Brief Return," "The Reason There Has Been World Peace Since June 4, 1968 – a fiction," "Grandchildren in the Pool," "Hot Day-Cool Dawn," "Double Double-Bonus"

Better than Starbucks: "Beginning, Wind's Considerations"

Big Windows Review: "Ghost Town"

Corvus Review: "Scholastic Poetry Award"

Down in the Dirt: "Spondylolisthesis Christmas," "Crash"

Gyroscope: "Phonebooth"

Ovunque Siamo: "Anthony," "Wedding Song"

Postcard Poems: "Heatwave," "I"

Right Hand Pointing: "Water Meter Reader," "Listen"

Soft Cartel: "2 a.m," "Rain in the Leaves," "Perfect Timing"

Southern Florida Poetry Review: "It's Not The Heat"

Third Wednesday: "Wind Quartet"

Verse-Virtual: "Flint," "Silent Dawn," "Layers – Rain, Feather, Pond" "'Time Heals All' —*That* Illusion" "My Father's Watch" "The first time I heard Lionel Hampton play I was seven years old and I was completely mesmerized not by the vibes but by his incredible vocalizations as if the music were so powerful that expressing it on his instrument was not nearly enough he had to vocalize it too"

As Boys do with their Farthings ... go to Heads or Tails for 'em.
—Thomas Otway, 1684

CONTENTS

Heads

High Mass Pass Out	17
Crash	18
The first time I heard Lionel Hampton play	
I was seven years old and I was completely mesmerized	
not by the vibes but by his incredible vocalizations as if	
the music were so powerful that expressing it on his	
instrument was not nearly enough he had to vocalize it too	19
Girls' Brigade Uniforms	20
I Still Wonder if Anyone Saw	21
Scholastic Poetry Award	22
Ghost Town	23
The Reason There Has Been World Peace Since April 8, 1968	24
Phonebooth	25
Water Meter Reader	26
Healing	27
Max Roach	28
Radio Personality	29
Fame?	30
Grandchildren in the Pool	31
Double Double-Bonus	32
My Father's Watch	33
Kelly, Outside Coventry Convenience – I	34
Kelly, Outside Coventry Convenience – II	35
Anthony	36

Spondylolisthesis Christmas	37
I Used to Be Able To…	38
"Time Heals All" — *That* Illusion	39
Flint	40
Wedding Song	41

Tails

Unapologetic Sentimentality	45
Pre Pre-Dawn	46
Heat's Brief Return	47
Hot Day – Cool Dawn	48
Heat Wave	49
Listen	50
It's Not the Heat…	51
Rain in the Leaves	52
2 a.m.	53
On Display Near the Window	54
Wind Quartet	55
Wind's Consideration	56
Birds Before Sunrise	57
Silent Dawn	58
Layers – Rain, Feather, Pond	59
Mantras	60
Fledglings	61
Something Chewed the Eggplant	62
Mushrooms	63
Pre-dawn Cardinal	64
I.	65

Before Rain, Before Dawn	66
Rain – 3. a.m.	67
Fata Morgana	68
Beginning	69
Notes on the Poems	71
About the Author	73

HEADS

High Mass Pass Out

Kneeling at the altar. High Mass. Father Shanley. My ears ringing like Sanctus Bells, but echoey. I touch my forehead. It's hot and sweaty.

Two lions pad across the altar, their low growl blending with the bells. Then, on the floor of the sacristy, Father calling, *Johnnie. Johnnie! Wake up!*

Crash

When the crotch-rocket t-boned the Toyota crossing 44, they said the bike was doing 150, ripped through the car, left the driver dead on the road, the biker severed, and you said one second you heard the bike scream by, and the next second you heard a sound like *poof.*

The first time I heard Lionel Hampton play I was seven years old and I was completely mesmerized not by the vibes but by his incredible vocalizations as if the music were so powerful that expressing it on his instrument was not nearly enough he had to vocalize it too

Ah! Ahah! Yeahyeahyeah! Ahahaha! Yeahhhh! Ahah! Yeahyeah! Yeahhhh-ahhh! Naaa! Ah! Ah! Ah! Hey! Ahahahaaaa! Ah! Aaah! Ah! Ahah! Ah! AH! Ahahahah! Ah! Yahahahahah!

Then still hypnotized I saw a blur of juggled drumsticks a whirling dazzling fire flare soaring bending chirring hurled around his smile a twirling whorl *Ah! Yeahahhhhh!*

Girls' Brigade Uniforms

St. Mary's School, 3rd Grade

Greg and I snuck into the Girl's Brigade storage room. I put on a uniform, cute blue skirt, white blouse with jabot, little cap.

Then Father entered, grabbed my throat, and hissed, *You snake!*

I've shed my skin a thousand times since that day, and there's always another snake inside.

I Still Wonder If Anyone Saw

I was a Little League star. Played first. *Throw the ball anywhere close, this kid's got it*, Coach says. And stretch? I could do a split.

Played one game with a rip in my pants. Stretched for a low throw and, horrified, felt the warm grass on my nuts.

Scholastic Poetry Award
1966

those days
seemed important
the pressure to fit it
was a hard road
when I won a poetry award
it proved I was a *faggot*
my legs were shaved

when football
and the confusion
to be cool
was hard won
overwhelming
I got jumped
by the guys on the team

Ghost Town
East Hartford, Connecticut, December, 1967

When I got home from Fort Dix, East Hartford was a ghost-town. Everyone was either working, at school, in Nam, or dead, so I'd spend long, bleak, suicidal afternoons in the woods naked, one hand on myself, one on my old man's shotgun, practicing being born, learning to die.

The Reason There Has Been World Peace Since April 4, 1968—*a fiction*

> Rev. Jesse Jackson called Dr. King's wife, Coretta, and said, "I think he's been shot in the shoulder." The reason he said this was because, as he said, "I couldn't say what I saw."

Children, here is what happened, an event so startling that a powerful and wondrous transformation flowed through all humanity; Dr. King was shot in the shoulder, and since that day, he has led all the people of the world to the profound peace and love you've known your whole lives.

Phonebooth

I found one of the phonebooths I used to call you from 40 years ago. It was in the white room of a museum, not connected to anything. It was just a "piece." When no one was looking I rushed inside and called you. When you answered I couldn't speak.

Water Meter Reader

In my 20s, I was a water meter reader. One day, when I was supposed to be reading meters, I was hiding in the library, reading *Othello*.

Summer flowed through the open window.

My brain got you all mixed up with Desdemona. I remember being blindsided by my own weeping.

Healing

       Can't hide pain from students. My knee hurt. Taught "Birches," recalling my youth.

       After class, a woman from Ghana asked, *May I pray on your knee?*

       She knelt. Bowed. Placed both hands on the knee. Chanted that the Lord heal me.

       After, my knee still hurt, but my spirit? Healed.

Max Roach

Newport Jazz Festival, August 16, 1992

  Rain on Newport Beach. Sherbet hats, umbrellas. Empty chairs. Max Roach teaching, playing, smiling, jazz ancestry in racing white clouds over white sails. Rhythms, polyrhythms, rolls, crashes, Philly Joe Jones tribute.

  Next to Max, there on the bandstand, a living creature, the high-hat, champs its toothless bit, a hysterical character.

Radio Personality

    This was a first. Twenty years at WHCN, the big rocker in Hartford, and threatening letters began arriving, addressed   *Johnithan Izzy—DJ*. Return address?— *Middle*.

    They consumed me. Shaky red handwriting, stained paper.

    Here's one. *You're stuck in my head, motherfucker. You're all the same. I'll find you!*

Fame?

Three rejections today! But one was not about the poems. I pissed off an editor on Facebook. Glad I watched *A Quiet Passion*—thought of Emily.

…If fame belonged to me, I could not escape her; if she did not, the longest day would pass me on the chase…

Grandchildren in the Pool

Come whenever you want! We don't have to be here!

A blessing—our house *theirs*.

Giddy summer laughter. Whirlpool wild. Too much fun to fight against. Waves of water over the side.

I feel peace when I get home, knowing that they've been here, pizza slices floating in the water.

Double Double-Bonus

> *But they that will be rich fall into temptation and a snare, and into many foolish and hurtful lusts, which drown men in destruction and perdition.*
> —1 Timothy 6:9-10 King James

Cashiers in Christmas garb. Muzak making my head hurt. Playing with house money. Not metaphorically. My *house* money. And BANG. A Royal. A $15 pull. Twelve grand.

Two hours later, busted. In the frigid car, I crank *Ticks and Leeches*, staring at the ice on the windshield melting to nothing.

My Father's Watch

I thought of it in a drawer, and believed, for a moment, that because it had been cast in darkness, its barrels would be empty, its jewels worn to nothing.

I had my father's watch repaired. $385. I couldn't afford it any more than I could afford *not* repairing it.

Kelly, Outside Coventry Convenience – I

Hi! Hi! she says, laughing, running place with tiny steps. *Do you pray? I pray twice a day, say, God, why am I alive? I don't know why I'm alive. Some guy drove into our motorcycle, me on the back. I was in a coma! Two fuckin' years!*

Fist bump.

Kelly, Outside Coventry Convenience – II

Orange sun-bleached hair to her waist. Pinkest rouge, thick and uneven halfway down her face. Her eyes are tiny, bloodshot and drunk behind a jungle of eyelashes crystallized with chunks of black makeup. She speaks like a toddler. Below her cheeks are burn-scars the texture and color of flank steak.

Anthony

Backyard football. You and me. Both *The* Giants. Me—Katcavage, Huff. You—Conerly, Gifford. We pounded each other.

Watched the Giants win the Super Bowl.

You got cancer.

Died.

Funeral home. Before it opened. You in a suit.

I looked you in the eyes.

Said, *What the fuck you doin'?*

Spondylolisthesis Christmas

The pain in my back is more exquisite than the brightest Christmas lights on the gaudiest house in town. My legs are numb to the soles of my feet. Can't put my socks on without agony, regardless of the *care* taken. Ruined Christmas for everyone.

For breakfast? Oxy and vodka.

I Used to Be Able to…

I all alone beweep my outcast state —William Shakespeare

Accept. Babble. Conceal. Desecrate. Exalt. Follow. Gyrate. Hallucinate. Justify. Knuckle. Long. Marginalize. Numb. Overpower. Persist. Quote. Resist. Seek. Tempt. Uproot. Visualize. Weather. Xfer. Yap. Zone.

Zero yearning. X-ray wafer vanished. Usually the summer rest quelled pain or nervousness. Memories' light knows Johnnie. Here genetics falter. Exhale. Dream. Cannot back away.

"Time Heals All" — *That* Illusion

As if your loss were made of colossal acres of black paper the edges too far to reach, too expansive, a continent, at nightfall. As if I could fold that continent into millions of origami birds that would soar up and out toward where the sky is beginning to brighten.

Flint

      Outside the town the cleft rested, small stationary arroyo, dried up pinhole too tiny for butterflies to roost.

      The villagers beaten down by Christ or images of love lost or never found, become silly when water is smuggled in, ash before it's poured, the destitute filling their cups with lies.

Wedding Song

Mikalah	Nick
always	remember
loving	the
sunshine	blessings
and	the
birds	singing
Mikalah	remember
Nick	weeping
loving	inexpressibly
the	mountains
grass	reaching
endlessly	the sun
brilliant	flowers
spirits	joyous
larger	symbols
than	emotions
words	and
Braelynne	luminous
little	life
reminder	that
love	blossoms
bringing	smiles
sweet	innocence
angelic	laughter

      devotion

TAILS

Unapologetic Sentimentality

Songs from within the motionless leaves, still as a painting, and the morning is steeped in wonder.

Quiet trees. Silent leaves. And the air from here to the pond is flourishing with birdsong, frog song, horse song, and a hushed quiet amplifying the landscape.

It can only be named *joy*!

Pre Pre-Dawn

       There are no lactic hooks or cracks in the flat black dawn, grayed through the screen grain—none, at least, that I can see. And if there are, I'd guess they're gently beveled, leavened against coronal ejections. And the sun's stepdaughter, the moon, only seems anemic, comedic geek, half-lit vagrant.

Heat's Brief Return

      Early heat as in the place where I should have been born, but was not born, and so I know I must wait impatiently for the slow frozen season to silk its way across the far landscape, bringing you to me finally, borne into your eyes again and then again.

Hot Day – Cool Dawn

       After complaining all winter about the cold, I complained all day yesterday about the heat. It was 91. But now, 4 a.m., dawn hints of smudging the night lighter. I hear a yellow warbler, oriole, cool wind. It's 63. Bottoms of leaves flash.

       Later I will tell you these things.

Heat Wave

Dare you see a Soul at the White Heat? —Emily Dickinson

90-plus for five days, and when I finally get the nerve to touch the wind, it's feverish.

Birds scream and pant. Tickseed sunflowers melt, spilling the color of lemonade onto the heated guests. The children's feet are stained yellow and each child is holding a drooped flower sequined with water.

Listen

That silent opening, spring, unlocks so gradually that it is not until the faded print of fall comes and goes with the same measured turning that we will say, *The birdsong we waited for, for what seemed like a lifetime, and that we didn't even hear arrive, is now gone.*

It's Not the Heat…

Humidity is unyielding, a force, that which holds the trees down by their shoulders or shakes them, fills shadows with fat, bloats bark, prompts birdsong to echo, frogs to stillness in warm shallows, and when rain comes, humid air breaks into pieces, and fills each droplet with a tiny cloud.

Rain in the Leaves

      Rain caught in the leaves is tenuous, each leaf dappled with crystal, a redundancy of little water globes, where, if we could, we'd see our own awestruck reflections in each drop, as the wind shakes out this bag of jewels on the languid river, with the sound of exhausted applause.

2 a.m.

      Day will become vast. Light opening. But now, after rain, it's black. Ground. Trees. Pondwater.

      In darkness, treefrogs fill their bubbles with love, stick to their trees, chanting.

      Thick stillness reaches in the window, touches the bark of my shoulders with its humid hands, might sing for me of summer.

On Display Near the Window

        The ceramic dog could not face the window, her eyes empty with the blankness of nightfall. Shadows and light redeployed, and the culverts chanted of the desolation tunnels. But what do shadows know about moaning, about the horror the Souls of the Faithful Departed must bear, wading knee-deep in night?

Wind Quartet

    Basso profundo bull frogs.

    Gulp thunk green frogs' percussive echoing.

    Rain playing the trees in a minor susurration.

    Miles says, *It's not the notes you play, it's the notes you don't play*.

    Here silence isn't silence, but a whole rest demonstrating the way to hold our breath anticipating a miracle.

Wind's Consideration

Ships creak over the land of the living, the dead.

The wind believes I should consider it alive and say,
See the leaves the breeze has birthed?

The wind's expectation is that I believe it's responsible for all movement,
even ships that navigate the arched crescent of the sparked darkness.

Birds Before Sunrise

      Unimaginable without them, the transition from night to dawn, darkness backlit by sun and mist. Well out beyond the tree-line, past the river, into the mountains, everything glimmers with their harmonies, the leaves holding their branches, the cool river beneath the heavy pastel of fog, all of it.

Silent Dawn

Some mornings birdsong is broadcast like notes in the dark. Every one invoking light. Barred owls' simian barks. The blue of the heron, symphonic as she awaits the least stir. The frogs' grunts thunk.

But this morning the only sound is the sound the dark makes when it is alone.

Layers—Rain, Feather, Pond

Drops of rain, spherical as mercury, on a white feather floating on the dark pond. The feather's gray border is magnified where rain has fallen, a tiny prismatic constellation, light on the galaxy of the pond. Here is where we live. Where we take form and, shivering, learn to fly.

Mantras

All during the incessant, brutal, silencing freeze this is what I dream—catbirds working all night lacing warmth into the chill—trills, chatters, squeaks, the cry of a cat that keeps small creatures wary.

And during the day, the mantra of a distant mower in the summer afternoon.

Fledglings

these spring
days when
birdsong leaves
and colors
solace are
vanished slowly
green stillness
past solely
quiet slow
and heartening
born into
frantic hunger
fledglings crowding
parents working
in concert
focus on
the hunger
feeding mouths
the only
concern these
pink beaks
open starving
and wings
fluttering wildly
dreaming free

Something Chewed the Eggplant

Where the landscape bends, water is prettier, flows unmuddied by the fatigue of deceits. And yes. Those *are* roses in the leftovers. They'll be fine uncovered in the ice box.

That racket is your timeline pounding.

No, I have not actually seen any slugs, but something is eating the garden.

Mushrooms

      A small priory of monks visited my garden to chant very quietly in the moonlight. I didn't even know they were there. I noticed them in their tiny, unsheltered abbey when I walked to the garden at dawn, basil at respectful attention, the eggplant bowing reverently in their purple vestments.

Pre-Dawn Cardinal

The fog and the tree tops bleed together, a watercolor, a dawn-softness that brings to mind kindness and the marvel of taking breath. It is 5 a.m. One cardinal has sung in the darkness since three. And finally the day tries to brighten on a landscape already magnificent with fog.

I.

> *From Cocoon forth a Butterfly*
> *As Lady from her Door*
> *Emerged—a Summer Afternoon—*
> *Repairing Everywhere—*
>   *—Emily Dickinson*

I wore shorts – informal –
Knew You would be gone –
Summer come – floral scent
Languid on the lawn –

I stood at Your Window –
Taking in Your view –
That's when – dressed in cabbage White –
Lilting wings of tulle –

A butterfly – spasmodic –
Dashing – in disguise –
Entirely hypnotic –
Saying You'd arrived –

Before Rain, Before Dawn

   Dawn—cardinals, catbirds, goldfinches, and a smattering of *cheers, cheers, here, right here!* Even the tree frogs have perfected bird song, trilling in the dark.

   And above and through it, the polyphonic advertisement of bullfrogs letting us know that the rain is closing in, and it's time for love.

Rain – 3 a.m.

      The cool sizzle of pre-dawn rain in the leaf-full trees, and so, just like that, memories of the heat-oppressed days wash away. Rain falls on the houses of the sleepers who will come slowly to hear it through their open windows, their eyes smiling in the dark at that sound.

Fata Morgana

standing on the edge of the sultry sea
                                        even the shade is hot
and fairy castles on the horizon
                bursting with poisonous raspberries
lure us to their warped doors
                              bent and ephemeral
and the Fata Morgana hovers for us
                            held up by heat
and our imaginations filled with stacked light

Beginning

      A tree-frog trills in the dark, echoing lightly in the midst of waning, a lighthouse of sound, a beacon of resonance that says, *Whether you come this way or not, dawn is here and brightening,* and a chorus of crickets passes through night's full tide, riding crest and trough toward light.

NOTES ON THE POEMS

Pages 22, 41, 61: *Scholastic Poetry Award*, *Wedding Song*, and *Fledglings* are written so that if you read them conventionally, left to right, they make sense. However, if you read only the left-hand column, top to bottom, it will also make sense – same with the right-hand column.

Page 20: *Girls' Brigade Uniforms* – The Girls' and Boys' Brigade were, in some ways, St. Mary's School's answer to Girl and Boy Scouts, only Catholic.

Page 29: *Radio Personality* – This stalking went on for well over a year. I received one letter a week, each more threatening and bizarre than the one from the previous week. Then the stalker made a mistake. One day a letter arrived on a piece of paper that had been torn in half. It was a letterhead of some sort; a few letters were visible, but also an entire phone number. I called the number and explained what had been transpiring. The woman on the other end of the phone was shocked. I had reached Connecticut Valley Hospital, the mental health facility in Middletown, Connecticut. The woman recognized the strange name this person had been using to sign his name as that of a patient. My voice had gotten stuck in his head and he decided he hated me. Hartford and Middletown police got involved, his doctors adjusted his meds, and the letters stopped coming.

Page 63: *Mushrooms* – The mushrooms were xeruloid mushrooms. I was amazed that in the afternoon there were no mushrooms in the garden. However, the very next morning, the garden beds were covered.

Page 65: *I.* – Visiting Emily Dickinson's homestead, I was standing at Emily's writing desk, looking out her window, when from behind a stone wall came a white butterfly! I was absolutely incredulous. There I was at Emily's desk, watching a white butterfly flit around on the lawn below, Emily's white dress on the mannequin behind me. It was one of the most extraordinary moments of my life. When I got home, Ms. Dickinson helped me to write the poem, 'I.'

Page 68: *Fata Morgana* – Fata Morgana is a form of mirage that is seen in a narrow band right above the horizon. It is the Italian name for the Arthurian sorceress Morgan le Fay. There is a belief that these mirages, often seen in the Strait of Messina, looked to sailors like fairy castles or land, and were created by le Fay's witchcraft to lure sailors to their deaths. A Fata Morgana may be seen on land or at sea, in polar regions, or in deserts.

ABOUT THE AUTHOR

John L. Stanizzi is author of the full-length collections: *Ecstasy Among Ghosts, Sleepwalking, Dance Against the Wall, After the Bell, Hallelujah Time!, High Tide – Ebb Tide*, and *Chants*. His poems have appeared in such publications as *Prairie Schooner, American Life in Poetry, The New York Quarterly, Paterson Literary Review, The Cortland Review, Rattle, Tar River Poetry, Rust & Moth, Connecticut River Review*, and *Hawk & Handsaw*. Stanizzi has been translated into Italian and appeared in *El Ghibli*, in the *Journal of Italian Translations Bonafinni*, and *Poetarium Silva*. His translator is Angela D'Ambra. He has read at venues all over New England, including the Mystic Arts Café, the Sunken Garden Poetry Festival, Hartford Stage, and many others. Stanizzi is the coordinator of the Fresh Voices Poetry Competition for Young Poets at Hill-Stead Museum, Farmington, Connecticut, and a teaching artist for the national recitation contest, Poetry Out Loud. A former New England Poet of the Year, named by the New England Association of Teachers of English, Stanizzi teaches literature at Manchester Community College and he lives with his wife, Carol, in Coventry, Connecticut.

www.ingramcontent.com/pod-product-compliance
Lightning Source LLC
Chambersburg PA
CBHW060427010526
44118CB00017B/2388